Higgle
Wiggle

POEMS BY EVE MERRIAM

Higgle Wiggle

Happy
Rhymes

PICTURES BY HANS WILHELM

A Mulberry Paperback Book New York

Watercolors were used for the full-color art.
The text type is 15.5 point Bembo.

Text copyright © 1994 by The Estate of Eve Merriam by Marian Reiner, Literary Executor.
Illustrations copyright © 1994 by Hans Wilhelm, Inc.

The Library of Congress has cataloged the Morrow Junior Books edition of *Higgle Wiggle* as follows:
Merriam, Eve. Higgle wiggle / Eve Merriam : illustrated by Hans Wilhelm. p. cm.
SUMMARY: A collection of short poems about various objects and animals, including mashed
potatoes, keys, and a bird in a sweet gum tree. ISBN 0-688-11948-4 (trade).—ISBN 0-688-11949-2 (lib.)
1. Children's poetry, American. [1. American poetry.] I. Wilhelm, Hans, ill. II. Title.
PS3525.E639H5 1994 811'.54—dc20 92-29795 CIP AC

3 5 7 9 10 8 6 4 2
First Mulberry Edition, 1995
ISBN 0-688-14547-7

Higgle Wiggle

Higgle wiggle piggy,
muddy as can be,
higgle wiggle try to
higgle wiggle catch me.

Higgle wiggle fish,
swimming in the sea,
higgle wiggle try to
higgle wiggle catch me.

Higgle wiggle monkey,
swinging in the tree,
higgle wiggle try to
higgle never catch me.

Tickle

Tickle a ladybug,
tickle a flea,
tickle a pickle,
but don't tickle me.

Tickle an elephant,
tickle a worm,
but please, oh, please
don't make me squirm.

Don't tickle my elbows,
my ankles or knees,
my shoulders or ears—
ah ha ha *ha* PLEASE!

Sidewalk Sounds

What's that
clip-clop,
clip-clop song?

Boots go
clomping,
stomping along.

What's that
quiet,
quiet hush?

Sneakers,
sneakers,
shush, shush, sh...

Sometimes

Pokey turtles
oh so slow.
Frisky rabbits
hop, jump, go.

Sometimes I'm a rabbit
and I run, run, run!
Sometimes I'm a turtle
stretching in the sun.

Quick, quick rabbit,
hop, jump, go.
Take it easy, turtle,
slow…slow…slow.

Secret

Open the door
with this key.

When people ask later,
"What did you see?"

Don't tell anyone,
not even me.

Home from the Beach

Take off your left shoe and shake it out—
sand, sand, lots of sand,
pots of sand.

Take off your right shoe and shake it out—
sand, sand, buckets of sand,
truckloads of sand.

Take off your left sock and shake it out—
sand, sand, piles of sand,
miles of sand.

Take off your right sock and shake it out—
sand, sand, fountains of sand,
mountains of sand.

Dump out your pockets,
thump out your pockets.
It's blowing sand,
it's snowing sand,
and look in your sun hat:
SAND!

Say

You say Crow
and I'll say Caw.
You say See
and I'll say Saw.

You say Frog
and I'll say Jump.
You say Ouch
and I'll say Bump.

You say Owl
and I'll say Who
Whooo whooo
hoo hooo hooo.

Mashed Potatoes

Mashed potatoes,
mashed potatoes,
piled up high,

mashed potatoes,
mashed potatoes,
up to the sky,

mashed potato clouds,
mashed potato moon,

scoop it all up
with a giant's spoon.

How to Be Angry

Scrunch your eyebrows
up to your hair,
pull on your chin
and glare glare glare,

puff out your cheeks,
puff puff puff,
then take a deep breath
and huff huff huff.

Dance

Dance out of bed,
dance on the floor,
dance down the hallway,
dance out the door.

Dance in the morning,
dance in the night,
dance till the new moon
is out of sight.

Dance all summer,
autumn and spring,
dance through the snowflakes
and don't forget to sing.

Lap Time

Kitten, little kitten,
climb onto my lap.
Kitten, little kitten,
how about a nap?

You slithered and stretched,
you quivered and prowled,
you leaped and scratched,
you howled and meowled.

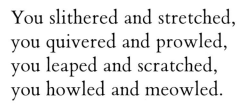

You hid in the closet,
you rumpled the bed,
you wrapped your sleeky self
all around my head.

You drank up your milk,
you licked your silky fur,
now fold in your paws
and purr, purr, purr.

What Is It?

It has no teeth,
so it can't eat a carrot.
It can't speak a word,
so it isn't a parrot.

It woggles and goggles
and scrunches its eyes.
It squawks and it yawps,
it burps and it cries.

It waggles its fingers,
it snuffles its nose.
Let's wait for a while
and watch how it grows.

Keys

Turn, turn,
turn about.
Turn your pockets
inside out.

Jingly jangle
tangle of keys.

Door keys,
store keys,
brass keys,
more keys,
trunk keys,
junk keys,
clink clank clunk keys.
Keys.
Keys.
Keys.

Banana, Banana

Banana, banana, banana, banana,
one bite for me and one for you.

Banana, banana, banana, banan—
banana's all gone, now what will we do?

No more for you, no more for me,
let's go climb a marshmallow tree.

In the Doghouse

It's nice and small,
my secret place,
and two can crawl
inside the space.

Rover makes
a furry rug,
while I give Rover
a snuggly hug

and we roll over
and over and o—
Rover, dear Rover,
don't snore in my face.

Bird, Bird, Bird

Bird, bird, bird
in the sweet gum tree,
la lee la,
lee la lee.

What is the song
you sing to me?
Is it la lee la
or lee la lee?

I wish I were a bird
in the sweet gum tree,
la lee la,
lee la lee.

Singing, singing
cheery as can be:
la lee la,
or lee la lee.

In the Kitchen

Pepper makes me sneeze:
kachoo! kachoo!
Onions make me cry:
boohoo, boohoo.

Farewell to pizzas,
burritos good–bye,
I'm going to bake
a shoofly pie.

Joan, Joan

Joan, Joan,
answer the phone.

Joan says, "It's not for me,
sounds like they want Lee."

Lee says, "Hello?
I think they're calling Joe."

Joe says, "What?
Wait a second for Dot."

Dot says, "Who?
Hold the line for Lou."

Lou says, "Yes?
I guess it's for Bess."

Bess can't tell if the call is for
Eleanor or Isadore

so she hands the phone to Joan.

Joan, Joan,
answer the phone....

Snuggle

Sweet bunny baby
at home in our hutch,
sweet bunny baby
soft to touch,
sweet bunny baby,
I love you so much.

Little bear baby
at home in our lair,
little bear baby
with soft fuzzy hair,
here's a bear hug
for my baby bear.

MMMMMM MMMMMMM

mmmm mmmmm
mmmm mmmmm

Come into the kitchen
and close your eyes.

mmmmmm mmmmmmm
mmmmmm mmmmmmmmm

You can tell that someone
is baking apple pies.

mmmmmmmm mmmmmmmm
mmmmmmmm *mmmmmmmmmm*

Smell the cinnamon
down to your toes.

mmmmmmmmmmmmmm mmmmmmmmmmm
mmmmmmmmmmmmmm MMMMMMMMMMMMMMMMM

What a delicious
time for a nose.

Downpour

In a spot   in a spat
in a spatter   a splat

in a soak   in a sop
in a plip   in a plop

in a dash   in a rush
in a splash   in a gush

in a gurgle   a glop
in a slippety slop

down pours the rain
drip drop drip drop...

Bath Time

Soap in the tub
slipple slapple slubble

Elbows and knees
scribble scrabble scrubble

Shampoo on head
bubble ubble bubble

Washcloth to squeeze
dribble dabble drubble

Water down the drain
spiggle spaggle spuggle

Water nearly gone
guggle uggle gluggle

Gurgle
      urgle
            gug

Counting

One for the rooster,
two for the hen,
three for the pig,
four for the pen.

Five for the garden,
six for the snail,
seven for the boat,
eight for the sail.

Nine for the bluebird,
ten for the nest,
and you are the one
I love the best.

Take a Look

Look out the window,
the sun's all gone.
Look at me,
I'm starting to yawn.

Look at the clock,
it's time for bed.
Look at me,
I'm nodding my head.

The stars are beginning
to shine in the skies.
Take a look for both of us,
I've closed my eyes.

Happy Dreams

I have a box
and in it I keep
a fleecy lambkin,
a woolly toy sheep.
It doesn't say Baa,
for it's fast asleep.

Next to the sheep
is a speckled toy fish.
It doesn't swim in
sparkling streams,
it's quietly dreaming
its own happy dreams.